POETRY of FRANCIS WARNER

POETRY
of
FRANCIS WARNER

*for ~~the~~ M. R. Lowe,
with all best wishes,
from Francis Warner.
April 8th 1970*

PILGRIM PRESS

PHILADELPHIA   BOSTON

SBN 8298–0153–7
Library of Congress Catalog Card Number 75–108761

Published by United Church Press
Philadelphia, Pennsylvania

for Margaret Kelley

CONTENTS

9   Acknowledgments

11   Experimental Sonnets

     1 Was that white shape that lurched out of the night 13
     2 A towel; suitcase; this a hotel room. 14
     3 As our fates navigate their destined route 15
     4 Night wins. The realizing dark 16
     5 As in her grief a mother cannot clean 17
     6 Outside, stuttering hate snarls down the blade 18
     7 Should we preserve intensity alone? 19
     8 If mechanism's throb betrays the mind 20
     9 The breaking dawn, the cry upon the bed; 21
     10 And can it be? Has all that splendour passed— 22

23   Plainsong

33   A Legend's Carol

41   Lyrical and Meditative Poems

     Lyric: When the wild 43
     Mankind's Mirror 44
     Byron's Pool 45
     For a Child 47
     Library Thought 48
     Fragment 49
     Threshold 50
     Lyric: Time passes 51
     Lyric: Sweetheart lie still 52
     Lyric: There is no splendour in the sun 53

Fondling Farewell 54
I Saw a Shining Lady 55
Venus and the Poet 56
Spell for Safe Return 57
Aubade 58
Song from "Lumen" 59
Womanhood 60
Unheard the Winds Blow 61
Close, Close Tight Buds 62
For Georgina 63
The Statues 64
Bells 65
The Truth 66
Hospital Dawn 67
The Ballad of Brendan Behan 68
West Coast Blues 70
East Coast Calypso 71
Song from "Emblems" 73

75 Perennia

ACKNOWLEDGMENTS

The poems in this volume have been selected from five previous books, and I should like to thank my English publishers for permission to present them in this form.

Perennia was first published by The Golden Head Press, Cambridge, in 1962; the two shorter poems "Fondling Farewell" and "I Saw a Shining Lady" were also published by the same press, in their anthology *Garland* in 1968.

With the exception of "Song from *Emblems*," all the others have previously appeared in one of the three collections of my work made by The Fortune Press, London—*Early Poems* (1964), *Experimental Sonnets* (1965), and *Madrigals* (1967).

I should also like to pay a debt of gratitude to those friends whose faith in my work has brought me to the New World on a number of extended tours across the continent; in particular to Olive Evans of *The New York Times;* Eunice Belgum of Harvard; Prof. Tom Parkinson, of the department of English, Berkeley; Prof. George Harper, chairman of the department of English, University of Florida, Gainsville; Prof. Vivian Mercier, of the University of Colorado, Boulder; Prof. Buckminster Fuller and Prof. Herbert Marshall, both of the University of Southern Illinois; Prof. Frank Kersnowski, of Trinity University, San Antonio; and Prof. David Ward of the University of Tulsa, Oklahoma.

To these I must add Dr. Tyrus and Dr. Kathleen Winter of St. Louis, and Dr. Robert and Mrs. O'Driscoll of St. Michael's College, Toronto, who have not only on many occasions made it possible for me to visit North America, but also—when weeks of readings, air travel and hospitality had taken their toll—provided me with the sanctuary of their homes for recuperation.

In thanking these I should also include all those whose homes have been my welcome on the fleeting visits such tours impose, not least my agent, Margaret Kelley, whose administrative genius has coordinated all, and whose encouragement has sustained an English pastoral poet catapulted into the jet set; to whom, as is only appropriate, this volume is dedicated.

Francis Warner
St. Peter's College
Oxford, England

EXPERIMENTAL SONNETS

1

Was that white shape that lurched out of the night
To suffocate our windscreen, breathing on
Into the perched and blinded loneliness
An owl? No prate of peopled England here.
The headlights catch the cautious rabbits' play
And romp them roadsiding, to widow past,
Unkiss the shroud and lift the latch of dark;
Probing the bosomed, catseyed mist ahead
Half-formed and damp; thick, intermittent, gone.
This far-past-midnight world of deerhorned trunks
And unrepentant fields so utterly ours
We tread the edge of promise with the dawn.
New senses register. Relive all these
As moving emblems of our sympathies.

2

A towel; suitcase; this a hotel room.
Each object, élite, curiously numb:
Clean, empty place of unreality,
All singly neat. Mad traffic hurtling on,
Metal, below. The bed's bare winding sheets.
Alone for time to come: then why sit down
To throw an understatement on a page—
How can I further explore heartbreak's pit
And come back sane? No: let the new scab form;
Stay numb. Cross-lock the door. Force the hand still;
Unless articulation stir, to fill
The icy moment at the heart of pain.
    Is there a reason behind human care?
    What is the acreage of its despair.

3

As our fates navigate their destined route
In modulations of intensity,
And times necessitate a change of time
Not in relationship but counterpoint;
As each new stroke is added by the brush
Of that practitioner of artistry,
And though we wear the cloak, yet do not know
The composition, or the epigraph;
As each new moment beats upon the pulse,
Let us resolve to try whatever comes,
Not in heat's self-paralysis of hate,
But with compassion's quiet certainty;
    And neither flinch, nor find across our course
    Memories of unmitigated remorse.

4

Night wins. The realizing dark
Granites that knife along eternity.
Who sins? What is this idle guilt?
Father forgive, by Thy Gethsemane.
Eat, drink, riot today and forget!
By Thine agony and bloody sweat—
Come, try at the wheel; spin, wager a bet!
Ransom my core from catastrophic debt.
If I must live with this full-earned abyss,
If I must face my moral holocaust,
Father, forgive, though I know what I do,
Forgive my sin against the Holy Ghost.
    The worst is done; the last brutality:
    And mine the sole responsibility.

5

As in her grief a mother cannot clean
The fingermarks left on the windowpane,
But finds relief in sitting for a while
Where he with deft impatience on the floor
Tugged off his shoes, still knotted by the fire;
Half-waits the tottering walk; picks up the coat
Dropped when fresh news was spilling to be shared
In nonsense-babbling talk of outstretched toy:
As at such times a father cloisters up
His thoughts, attempts to play the comforter,
Awkwardly; climbs beneath the roof to search
For papers that he knows may not be there:
　　As such emotion dreads to be betrayed,
　　So, in the silent grief, one part's afraid.

6

Outside, stuttering hate snarls down the blade
As a pneumatic drill rapes the dead quay:
Inside recreated, as a shaft
Of black light penetrates the opened soul.
Somewhere a plumber saws his piece of lead;
A ribbed and creaking boat heels on the sand;
Nearer, a drawing-pin studs in the eye
Of mind, as vessel, float, all disappear.
Down, down as they go, the bubbles rise,
The drowned's report upon experience.
Up, up expanding hope replies
Until exploded by the drill's retort.
  Ah, comedy divine, man's tragedy—
  Why make us gambol in our agony?

7

Should we preserve intensity alone?
The string vibrating at the cello's bridge?
Or stretch to nerve the fingerboard's full range
In orchestrating waste's cacophonics?
Is poignancy of beauty's transience
As time runs over an apple in the stream—
The hesitancy of a summer's dusk
When nightstock stuns with scent—ours to forego?
Must we desert court-ladies on the grass
Their sunlit-dappled breasts and lovers' lutes?
The skill of craftsman-wrought, firm, rounded themes;
The guests of Mozart, Purcell and Watteau?
     Bear with me if I leave such scenes behind:
     The dark offstage preoccupies my mind.

8

If mechanism's throb betrays the mind
But once, then restless empiry's collapsed;
The vermin rob immortal artistry
And wisdom, fleshless, reels into the dust.
Grey waste of intricacy's heritage
Endowed to growth and destined to decay
Disburses melody, like pollen blown,
Loath to depart yet powerless to stay.
Abrasive anger at such impotence
To help the frailer by diviner part
Engineers atrophy of maimed desire
And nails inevitable reconciled.
    So dialectics isolate the flaw.
    So small a key unlocks so great a door.

9

The breaking dawn, the cry upon the bed;
Tottering infancy and gangling youth;
Mandarin manhood. Anarchy of age
At last, raving, forlorn and groping back,
Fearing the icy wind's strangling grip,
To corridors of constant journeying;
The secret prides and flattering self-denials;
Laconic labials, fantasy's deceit;
Books, Bibles, bidets; halls, hills, cottages;
Flow and ebb of bodily seasons' tides;
Those motley macaronics day and night;
Companions—all the panoply of rust.
    No intermission from this pantomime
    Till termination bring an end to time.

10

And can it be? Has all that splendour passed—
Was it too pure for weak mortality?
Was I demanding, hoping it might last;
Now disillusioned with humanity?
It seems impossible so firm a joy
A love so rooted, in a summer's day
Shared tasks, shared wanderings, should like a toy
A child has wearied of be tossed away.
And can this paper be the last that you
Will hold of mine, these words end passion's qualms?
Darkness must touch these eyes now, as we knew,
And lonely nights lend you their empty arms.
    Strange how the mutability of things
    Evaporates all man's imaginings.

PLAINSONG

PLAINSONG

**In memory of
Angus and David**

"Reapt ere half ripe, finisht ere half begunne."

A viper's cored within this apple-world,
And sunning through the orchards of the mind
Choosing only the red and ripest fruit—
The bruised ignored, the bitter thrown aside—
No more tells true; it satisfies no more.
A second's dead. Two warm and living friends
Wasting in mud and loam: suddenly snuffed
On reaching manhood. One, and now another.
Why, why oh why is this bitterness of doubt,
This thud of guilt and loneliness of despair,
Impossible, titanic weight of a universe
Balanced to try each one of us in turn?

I must not pose, colour or decorate
And clothe an ugly fact: lament Adonis,
Or mourn on Lycidas's golden urn.
As memory grows distortion will encroach,
And the brute impact of shattering moment on soul
Borne in the heart alone, but labelled sorrow
Will fade: yet while it cuts into my brain
I'll make a map of torment; bend the verse
And wrest from it an iron ore of truth
Stripped of accretions made from imitations:
Lift up that flap of the brain and journey in
To grip the bit and bridle of the heart.

I've said I'll strike no attitude—and yet
Saying that may itself be one more pose
No truer than those first ones stripped away:
Or do I like, enjoy the sound of grief
And say I say I mourn? Away, mind-spider!
This creeping ivy's curst. I doubt my doubts,
And meanings have no meaning when intellect
Battens on raw emotion: one more way
Creation tries to hide, to shift the burden
Seeking a screen in arguments on terms,
Fleeing the core and crawling round the skin
Wide of the bitter heritage within.

Sorrow humiliates, is hard to bear
Because the mightiest structures of the mind
Prove groundless; vanish in a puff of smoke:
And puny man retaliates in grief
Throwing his weightiest words in the empty air;
A whistling ant on an orange. Banished from home,
His comforting illusions swept away,
His petty pride and patronage destroyed,
He faces the unknown—yet still re-forms
Newer delusions for those cut apart
When shock shewed all had lied. The spear of fear
Burns to the bone until he builds once more.

Anatomies of grief, wild posturings,
Word-spun distractions, analytic sleights,
Convention and invention breeding still
Unfelt belief, untested promises—
All wrestling factions in the dark extreme
Passed by—attention drawn away with skill
To surface crusts spanning the torn abyss:
These are mere tricks; mirrors in place of glass,
Telling no more than happiness requires;
Puppets of showmen fanning childhood thoughts
With idle tales by hayricks in the sun;
Bolting the door that opens on the void.

To realize each moment as it comes,
Naked, for what it is, will be my task.
This chair set back within a book-lined room,
That creaking movement of the tree outside
Stripped to its branches while the wind blows cold;
A dust-filled crack between two flooring boards:
The crow on the roof. Tomorrow will be spring,
Yet grey-white clouds are piling in the sky
Like down: the snow is staying late this year,
And dusk soon falls. No proof has come of spring,
No swarming crowds of peewits in the fields:
Only this hollow deadness in my chest.

And yet some night ago I sat just here
Gazing out through this window.   Then the dawn
Had scarcely touched the sky.   Faint, earliest light
Tipped the trees white and froze each hedge and bush
With needle-blue of frosted handiwork.
The scarecrow on his crutch was crisp with cold,
And water butts stood shackled in thick ice.
Slowly full day had spread across the sky
Freeing the water from the chilled spring-well,
Filling each wood with life and waking cocks
Till far away a homing owl had called
His cry that silent slaughtering was done.

Then all was fresh.   Imagination clothed
Each fact of nature in its simplest joy.
No irons had been heated for the soul;
No snare or mesh had sprung and trapped the pulse
Each single creature woke inside my heart.
Now evening blows and sleet begins to fall
And I must force corroding images
Away, lest grief becomes a luxury.
Daylight has nearly gone, yet clear outside
A cart-track runs: a course that I must take.
The window's dark.   A dead leaf taps the glass.
I'll drag myself alone into the night.

Cold lashes strike my face.   The track is hard
And slippery; storm wind cuts through my hair
In rifts while far away dim city lights
Beckon me on like fishing lamps at sea.
Storms in my mind should cease while icy gusts
Hold well at bay all but immediate thoughts—
Dark hollows full of weeds, my sodden hair,
This bitter rain and massacre of wind:
Music of elements that scours the soul
And makes the muscles pull their proper strength.
This blast will clear my brain and fight the growth
Of weird embellishments that breed despair.

Dark of the soul, darkness soul-bright:
The image echoing-chamber of the mind
Twisted in cramp that tightens its clamp—
Tear-blind in sight of its goal.

Numb to the battering wind
Oblivious of pain
Only the dead beat in the head
And images that fight
Contorted, grotesque, like shadows that camp-fire the night.

On to the distant lights
Though canvas stretches till split;
Heaven torn as a world is stillborn
And hatred of gods gutters our phantom out.
The dragon of night burns the bridges and torments the trees
Which shoulder a burden that cracks on the traveller's knees.

Shelter of buildings; city streets at last:
Landscape of suffering worse than my own.
Man-made mortality. This chapel door
With guildings marked in subtle filigree
Will shield from buffeting. From the far end
Boyish vitality soars to the roof
Worrying out each sleeping spider's web.
The climbing words sink down into my ears
Like silkworms, calling, "He that shall endure
To the end. . . ." A leech has slipped down on my sleeve
And thirds descending end the anthem's tale.
Once more I'll fight the bawling wind and hail.

This is the city boundary, where the lamps
And houses cluster in one final knot
That's flattered with a flower-bedded tree.
On, blustering strides! Have pity on the lambs
Born on the fen. Muster your forces for
An onslaught on the coffin-leaded laws
That rule this meaningless and cancered globe
In socket-eyed, gigantic merriment
Like grinning cormorants with new-hatched eggs,
Or madmen leaning on a laddered man
Who gazes frantic at the swimming ground
While stifling heart-pants cataract his eyes.

The railway crossing. Now the fen itself
Stretches out like a glacier of ooze
Waded by buried gods, who shake their hill
With sleepless tossing and dream-stifled fears
And trudge the peat beyond the dyke in storms
Drinking in serried darkness like a draught
That drunken demons throw across the sun
Blanketing clouds to rifle virgin souls
Who sink in fear before their tyrant strength.
The piping gleemen of the tempest-dance
Shrouding the earth and waking walrus-wastes
Hunt down the deer that streaks across the sky.

I know a lonely inn where two streams meet
To make a river, where a goat is tied;
A ferry moors; and broken window frames
Offer their thin resistance to the storm:
Unsheltered coltsfoot shiver on the bank,
And bindweed claws and chokes the fishy reeds.
Now that the wind has held its breath, I'll make
My way there; try to find pure solitude,
That silent space of quiet that enfolds
The vacuum kingdom of the realm within;
Far from all cry of crippling appetites
That race exhausted blood about the veins;

And cool this cook and windmill of a mind
A moment, thinking of past summer days
Spent by that inn, when silver willows grew
Across a brook dense with strange riverweeds;
Watching a stickleback weave in and round
Hover, and flick his fin, while sun-hard clay
Gleamed brick-white when soft winds blew corn in lanes.
The sleeping snail that sunbathed on a log;
The vole that held a twig between his teeth
Keeping it dry aloft, as on he swam
Steered by his heirloom tail: the crickets' cry;
The fledgling that rebelled and lost his life:

The widening sky that served the setting sun
Platformed like polished tables from a feast
Of dazed and drunken ancient deities,
When healths pledged high, and crimson wine spilled down

Tracing bold, airy fables of past days,
Blazing a tapestry for creeping man.
So often I have knelt to watch a plant
Or insect, or a tiny animal,
Zoo-beast or meadow-grazer, fish or fly,
And known I felt with every living growth
That feels: a shiny toad or woolly sheep.
Cruelty razor-cut my arteries.

The lonely fens are dark tonight
    And swept by wind and rain.
The watcher in the lonely house
    Deaf to the windowpane.

A wanderer with a hurricane lamp
    Moves by the river side.
A mother mourns in the candlelight
    Silent and glassy-eyed.

She's laid his naked body out
    And lit the candles round.
The blackened river swells outside:
    Her mourning makes no sound.

"Halloo! Come, open up the door!
    The rain has pierced my skin!"
With fingers numb of feeling
    She lets the traveller in.

"These many hours I've watched with you
    Yet still the wicks burn bright!"
"I gave you shelter from the storm:
    Watch till the morning light."

The lonely fens are desolate
    The house but bricks and straw,
And empty winds throughout that house
    Will blow for evermore.

This ferryboat must do—where are the oars?
Away from this derelict ghost-haunted inn
And mourning candle-glow. The dawn is queer:
No breeze. The goat's stopped munching. Now's the time

When geese stretch up to hiss, and distant bells
Sound clearer; cocks crow; soot falls in the fire,
And cats wash back their ears. Rain's on the way
And I alone within this little boat,
Oarless, and bitterly tired. You bulrushes,
Bearded and wrapped with fears that weigh you down,
Give me your blessing. Stones and swiftest birds
If I must suffer still, defiled within,

Broken and beaten, give me power to bear
All that must come! My coward body shakes
And water smears my eyes in molten glass.
This speeding, wheaten, clay-gold river speeds,
Carries me on. The drumbeat in my eyes
Frightens me. Every world-born life that dies
Is not forced to endure this cruel sport
Of elemental kings whose thumbs turn down!
What is the index to your catalogue
Of punishment? Are fuel faggots still
To come in sacramental sacrifice,
My victim reflex analysed in fire?

The thoughts of love in a whirlwind
Cry out from the antique shore
To strike the nerve of the heart of man for evermore.

The cries of the frozen sparrow
Pinched in spears of snow
Waste in the winding winds where the arctic mirrors blow.

Half through our life, half through our dark,
Gusts on the flickering fen—
The madness of wind and storm scatters the breath of men.

What is that speck in the north? That growing cloud
Approaching, blackening the air? The midnight bull
Mighty, primeval, bursting from the sky
To butt this worthless bubble globe aside
Trampling the fair and circus of mankind
Like clover in a field: thirsting for death
His horns rip up the heavens and cyclones swoop
Wresting up trees and rocks, swamping the land
Beneath a sheet of sea. Towers tottering

Bend and crash. A ship splits down its back
Though still this nutshell boat flees in the vast
Ungovernable splendour of the storm.

The contemplation of a universe
In chaos is the holocaust of joy
And hatred, fear, pride, laughter, pain
Clear vision of destruction vouched to this
Trans-sanity. All things boast equal terms
Beneath the unchaining elements that strain,
Rage, and batter this defenceless earth.
Titanic battle of giant squid and whale
In lonely ice-wastes down the winter nights,
Monsters that scatter snowcaps, shrink in size
To a thimble where two pliant gnats make love
Measured beside this crown of final death.

The sun on the broken mountain blesses the final sea
That washes away the muddy foam of man-made futility.
The devastating and recreating waters that cover the earth
Promise a new healing refreshment for elemental dearth.
A mighty view of sun, season, earth, sea, and sky
Bound in one chain of perfect love, joyous that man must die,
Sends out a silent, ageless oath: that the new will be undefiled,
And all the archaic world unknown in the joy of their newborn child.

Cambridge, March 1962

A LEGEND'S CAROL

A LEGEND'S CAROL

for Roger Martin

The air was purified with frost,
And many a lonely mariner lost
    Upon the sea
Raised a numb hand to shield his sight,
And stared up at the starry night
    In reverie;
While far away, in from the shore,
  Ice on the roadside wells
Thickened, and snowdrifts round each door
  Deadened the cattle bells.
      The sleeper shrank deeper
      And pulled his blankets high,
      While burrow and furrow
      Lay still beneath the sky.

A crowd of drunken revellers
Laughed at a pair of travellers
    Who called for room.
They mocked the man for his grey hair
And jeered at what they saw her bear
    Within her womb:
"Are you that old man's wife?" they said
  "Who made you fatten so?"
But Mary simply bowed her head
  And went out in the snow.
      Then gladly, yet sadly,
      They left the inn behind,
      While jeering and sneering
      The others drank and dined.

Then Mary whispered in his ear,
She felt her time of birth was near
    And shook with cold.
Splinters of ice hung from the trees
Creaking like guilty memories
    Of crimes untold.
They passed a cave beside the road
    Where bullocks froze in sleep
While crisp outside the starlight glowed
    Upon a midden heap.
        But tearful and fearful
        She throbbed within her gown:
        So gently, intently,
        He lifted Mary down.

Leading their donkey to the cave
They took the shelter that it gave
    For Mary's bed;
And gathering her road-stained dress
She lay within a rock recess
    Where straw was spread.
Then stable animals drew round
    To keep her body warm
While hard across the frozen ground
    Jolted old Joseph's form.
        Both riding and sliding
        Along the hardened track
        He worried, and hurried
        To bring a midwife back.

The busy town was wide awake,
And Joseph had to shout to make
    His message clear;
For Caesar had proclaimed from Rome
Each should return to his own home
    From far and near
To be enrolled; and streets thick-packed
  With bodies barred his way
Till an old nurse, her voice age-cracked,
  Heard what he had to say.
    Then hearing, and fearing
    Lest Mary came to harm,
    She scolded, and folded
    Some blankets on her arm.

But when they came back to the hill
A blinding cloud came down to fill
    The cave with light
And dazzled them, until at last
The flame, its blaze of fury passed,
    Shone clear and bright.
They trembled like two hawthorn clumps
  That waver on a dyke
Where willows pollarded to stumps
  Bend for a lightning strike.
    But shaking and waking
    They found her undistressed;
    For sweetly, discreetly,
    Her baby sucked her breast.

Some streaks of day spread through the sky
As Mary sang a lullaby
        To her newborn.
Linnets and starlings perched around
Waking all nature with their sound
        And din of dawn:
The orchards and the olive-groves
        Filled with fresh-waking noise,
And early cattle passed in droves
    Driven by sleepy boys.
            Then tramping and stamping
            Some shepherds asked if they
            Might enter; they sent her
            A lamb this holy-day.

One star remained, although the sun
Softened the snow-webs night had spun,
        When from the East
Out of the dawn, like ripened grain
Rippling a field, a camel train
        Thundered, released
From wandering and pilgrimage,
    For now three men appeared;
One young, one silvery with age,
    One dark, with uncut beard.
            Descending and bending
            To enter with their store
            Of treasure, with pleasure
            They spread it on the floor.

Symbols of royal gods of old,
Time-honoured mysteries untold
    And myrrh of death
Surrounded Jesus where he played,
While gulls and meadow pipits strayed
    Catching their breath
In chokes of song; and Mary gazed
    Too full with happiness
To speak, while Joseph stood amazed
    Staring and motionless.
        Now sweeping and keeping
        The cave from mud and mire,
        With cinder and tinder
        The shepherds made a fire.

When evening came a hidden breeze
Wafted within a swarm of bees
    That filled the air
With sounds that seemed to sink and swell,
Like music in an ocean shell
    Or badger's lair.
A shadow hovered, still, outside
    As though afraid to come,
Until at length it ceased to hide:
    And the bees ceased to hum.
        Then, wary, a hairy
        Rough form came from the street,
        And listful, yet wistful,
        Laid reed-pipes at his feet.

And late that night, when all had left,
A helmsman nodding on his chest
   Woke with alarm:
A sudden wind from off the shore
Beat on his sails a bitter roar
   That broke the calm.
He saw his rigging torn away
   And left without a shred,
And heard a loud lamenting say,
   "Tell out great Pan is dead!"
      Then swirling and hurling
      Its thunder of that name,
      With calling and falling
      The wind sank as it came.

Cambridge, February 1962

LYRICAL AND MEDITATIVE POEMS

LYRIC

When the wild
Rose is snapped,
And the child
Caught and trapped,
When the hare
Is crushed in the road,
A mental snare
Starts to corrode.

Love is beyond
The worldly man.
Marriage bond
Of Pot and Pan
Is a pale
Mockery;
Lifelong stale
Lechery.

Death's a brave
Ranting shout
In an empty cave;
Life gutters out.
Limbs of an antelope
Stretched in the grass
Make us grope
For the mountain pass.

When the slender
Primrose shoot
Pushing tender
Underfoot
Makes the child
Leap in the womb;
Then undefiled
Will the wild rose bloom.

MANKIND'S MIRROR

The shadow moves on the wall. Ambivalence
Of image. Sun, or moving finger? Still
It moves in meditative patience—
A concrete myth; intangible, yet real
As knocker on a door, or hammered nail.
Why does it move so inexorably?
As though it knows all that mankind can feel,
And knowing, does not pause; but each detail
Of our existence reckons up, absorbs
Into itself; and still moves on; the weight
Of Calvary and of Hiroshima
And all the killing that makes up the freight
Of human history. Unshaped, and silent,
Still persevering on across the wall;
Neither a thing, nor god, nor animal:
Just a petitioner for penitence.

BYRON'S POOL

Beside a field of corn, this tangled wood
Wakens to life at dusk; the trees around
Rustle in the evening air, and welcome home
The rooks and crows, the nightjars, magpies, wrens,
Squirrels, and all the host of animals
That live among their branches and their roots.
Nothing is still: the whole wood breathes and feels;
A water-vole runs through the undergrowth
And drops in the stream; a noisy pigeon calls
His fourfold, clownish cry.   Numberless insects
Swarm round my head; and where I sit, a stump
Hollow with damp and age holds giant fungus.
Green leaves lie all around rich with the scent
Of wet and evening—sycamore and beech,
Elder and lime.   One tatter'd oak leaf falls.
A hawthorn tree breaks its spiked reflection
In the swirling river, as it leans from the bank
And sways its twisted trunk.

                              High overhead
Rustle of branches merges with the rush
Of water on the weir; and to the west
Streaks of fantastic sunset hover still
Over the cottages of Grantchester,
While by the church beyond the cornfield
The moon is full and low over the barns
That store the harness, sugar beet, and grain.
Darkness grows, and still my ears are full
With multitudes of sounds.   Slowly the smell
Of mist creeps from the fields.   Two new-hatched owls
Call, and there comes a hedgehog scuffling twigs,
Oblivious to me and all around him.
On flows a swan, with cygnets like herself,
But brown; on, past the weir.   Bats play in the air,
Moths flirt with the river; a fish dives up
For a gnat, and leaves circles of water rippling
Outwards and outwards till they fade in weeds.
Hollows and humps in the ground take on new shapes
And shadows.   Night transfigures all the wood.

The feel of darker beasts that search for prey
Pervades. Beetles are still: the hedgehog's gone:
The swans have passed; and on the leaves above
Patters the sound of the first midnight rain.

FOR A CHILD

I saw a squirrel on a tree,
And he laughing said to me
"Funny human, tell me why
You are so afraid to die?"

"Little squirrel," I replied,
"Many, many folk have died;
Yet not one's come back to me
Proving immortality."

"Timid mortal," said my friend,
"Do you think that death's the end?
Know the acorn, when it dies,
Doubts an oak tree will arise.

" 'How could such a mighty tree
Spring from nut so small as me?'
For the acorn does not know
Where it grew, or what will grow.

"If you cultivate your shell
And starve the kernel in its cell,
When the earth gives you her bed,
Your true part is maggoted.

"You are sleeping in this life
In a shadow world of strife;
Yet when the dream grows old and lame
You will wake to life again."

"Thank you, gentle squirrel. I
Am no more afraid to die."
And, not wanting to seem rude,
I threw him a nut in gratitude.

LIBRARY THOUGHT

I sit at an old desk, among old books
Within a garret—a low-ceilinged, dusty
Attic; and the breeze-blown sun outside
Scarcely bothers to search these little windows
Leaded in diamond shape, thick-smoked, with husks
Embedded in the glaze: but my attention
Drifts from my writing to that sudden buzzing,
A hectic fly that's climbing round the leads
Insulted by invisible blockade,
Infuriated; stamping all six feet
And grumbling at the unattending sun.

What perseverance. Up he goes again
A little hungrier, more tired now
But still determined: wife at home no doubt,
Waiting his manly strut, deep-throated buzz,
The busy hum of his acquaintances
As they sip gathered nectar of an evening
Setting the world to rights. The old and frailer
One by one failing to call at dusk
Around the tenement built of three straws
Under the thatch. These start to shade his thoughts.
He is but in the very stride of life—
He fail to return? Unthinkable
(Could that time come? Absurd.) No. Tries again.
Pause for a rest. The children! Up, and leaves
The window, racing round the dusty shelves
And back; back to that one small piece of glass.

My angry, tiny friend; I feel the same
Absent from her: I'll let you out again.

FRAGMENT

In these volcanic, seething days
Of enemies, uncertainty,
Deception, insincerity,
And turning twenty thousand ways

To grasp some foothold on this rock,
The drop below, vultures above,
One constant's certain as the clock;
Our mutual agony of love.

THRESHOLD

A brutal trace across an adolescent sky,
  And boyhood's gone.
A slight, sophisticated touch of mockery,
  And where there shone
The eagerness, the trusting faith of youth,
The natural fearlessness and confidence
That every man when shown must love the truth—
This glowing optimism of ideals
Reels, and is snuffed by adult common sense.

Those questions are not easy, cannot be
  Solved in a statement
The fugue must weave greater complexity
Of new experience upon old themes of doubt, piling, till spent
In questionings the resolution comes,
Stating again, in deeper majesty,
Those hard-won bars afresh, while muffled drums
Approach to turn the page, and silence all the resonance of breath.

LYRIC

Time passes,
Youth flies away;
The greenest grasses
Soon are hay.

That bunch of straw
Is last year's nest,
And woodworms gnaw
The lavender chest.

Her eyes were brown,
Her lips were soft,
Her cheeks like down
The dew has washed.

We laughed and played
And loved our fill:
Till dusk we stayed
On Madingley Hill.

An acorn grows;
Is felled at last.
The west wind blows,
And the hill stands fast.

LYRIC

Sweetheart lie still, that's not the sun
Touching the sky, dawn's not begun;
Sweetheart lie still, no night is passed
While we are tight like oysters clasped.

Darling, no daylight streaks the wall
Over our bodies, no birds call:
Ghosts of lovers unborn and dead
Shroud tomorrow from this bed.

Freshest bread needs freshest leaven,
Saplings will spring up anew;
Born we are in rain from heaven,
Rise again in morning dew.

LYRIC

There is no splendour in the sun
While you are absent from my arms,
And though I search till day is done
Remission in oblivion
Watching the busy crowd go past,
Driving the brain, callousing palms,
No high philosophy rings true
Nor can contentment come, till you
Bring peace of mind, and rest at last.

FONDLING FAREWELL

Fondling farewell, have done with dalliance
Urgent and young, you need far more than me.
Splendour and fame must claim their recompense
And wide ambitions have their larger sea—
    Those gentle hours that you and I have known
    Fade into thoughts that linger when alone.

Go on your way, soft hands, the world is yours,
Geography encircle with a flight
Till lands that lie beneath, nations' applause
Dazzle acclaim and take my sole delight.
    High star of fortune, sail where you are sent:
    Fondling farewell, but farewell too content.

I SAW A SHINING LADY

I saw a shining lady stand
In fields I could not recognize.
Caught unawares in a strange land
I stared at where her path would rise
 Across a nettled wilderness
 Shadowing ruin's emptiness.

I saw her walk on crumbling rocks
(How near to heaven I could not gauge)
But softening her barefoot shocks
Five-petalled meadow-saxifrage
 Wove yellow buttons and long stems,
 Like buttercups beside the Thames.

The red herb-Robert twined a bridge
With celandine and town-hall-clocks
Across the hard, uneven ridge
That marked decay of walls and locks,
 Roof, windows, bricks turned back to loam
 That constituted once a home.

And all my heart was filled with light
To see how she was safely held,
The stones themselves stirred with delight
And tears behind my eyelids welled.
 But when they cleared once more I found
 The Oxford traffic all around.

VENUS AND THE POET

He: Is there future in the past
Hazard once the die is cast?
Or in parting can there be
Dying immortality
From chance words that yet remain,
Evanescence in a stain?

Must a circumstantial blow
Murder what was born to grow
While the passing wintry days
Echo "All decays, betrays . . ."?
Love and poetry sustain
Small defence against the rain.

She: Come, leave mutability,
Lie me down beneath this tree;
Surging spring laughs doubts to flight
Strength increases with delight
Till, where Absence long has lain,
My lover reaps his ripened grain.

SPELL FOR SAFE RETURN

Stay, waves, stay, cease your inconstant crying
Trace no increasing tears upon the sand,
Fall, winds, fall, buffet no more with sighing
But bring my darling safely to my hand.

Reach, song, reach over remorseless breakers
Straight as a gannet skim through the sea-wind's whips,
Find out her furrows, music's unblemished makers,
Pearl the disturbing dew between her lips.

Fathomless sunbeams, sweep through the secret ranges
Coralled and shelled, waken them with your heat,
Drag up the seabed, scattering all that estranges
Till shipwrecked skulls form cobbles for her feet.

Carry my calling, echo through vaults of the ocean,
Far through the faint horizon's evening mist,
On, till the restless violence of this potion
Still urging sleeplessness like bodies kissed.

AUBADE

1

Hush! Who is that disturbs my leaden rest
    Startling the lark?
Who makes me let the night winds feel my breast
    Calling from whispered danger of this garden?
Are you foolhardy? Reckless of all . . . Hark!
    He moves in the next room: there'll be no pardon.
Ah Love, since love has lit through miles and darkness to you
Warm me within your naked bed that I may woo you.

2

My firm request you should not seek me here
    You disobey!
Your beauty overwhelmed numb caution's fear;
    Give me the penalty such wrong incurs
Prison me in your arms, condemn to stay
    Now I am in and not a hedgehog stirs.
Ah sweet unwise, so strong to take your own possession
Gentle me till the furthest star spills our confession.

3

Tenderest safety ends, the East grows light
    Dress and depart;
Dally no more, but vanish with the night
    Stay not to risk the terrors of the dawn,
Ring not a harebell, though you've wrung my heart,
    Nor break the melting cobwebs on the lawn.
Ah that I could sleep out all time till our next meeting;
For joy, though crown of all, is transitory, fleeting.

SONG FROM "LUMEN"

Bright apricot, kissed by the sun
And bulrush blest,
Lulled by the ripples of still yielding springs
Stretch out, my sweet
All is discreet
Here, where the easy strength of summer's heat
Leaf-lifts a shade
Of dappled willow branches I have made
Through which your skin, caressed, unharmed, may drink
The glory of the world until it sink.

Then, as dusk curls
His shimmering smoke-light round the apple trees
And plucks each stem with darkness from its bough
Then come with me
Warm in anticipation's tensity
Where only windowed moonlight's eye can pry
Upon such secrecies
Disclosed in flower-filled summer's stroking breeze
As make night fall
And our soft bird his breathing song of bridal call.

WOMANHOOD

Womanhood washed and warm
Delays before her image in the glass
Held by her form;
Deaf to the storm
That rifts and stabs the full clouds as they pass;
Only aware of wonder in the air
Feeling her breasts unbounded and her body bare.

Come my spring dawn with sunbreak in your eyes,
Bud freshly blown, flower that no frosts destroy,
Beauty incarnate in her own surprise
And made a woman in a night of joy,

Division yields to dewfall when we play
Discords resolve on music of your kiss
Your petals turn and open to my day
And all the storms of life are lost in this.

UNHEARD THE WINDS BLOW

The thorn on the briar
   Hangs fresh after rain.
If love light so seldom
   It comes not again.

Curled close like a child
   Asleep after play
Like eyebright in meadow
   At close of the day.

No sound but her breathing
   Breaking the calm
Still as a baby
   At breast in my arm.

Unheeding beside me
   Unheard the winds blow
As peacefully sleeping
   As starlight on snow.

CLOSE, CLOSE TIGHT BUDS

Close, close tight buds now parting ends the day
    Laughter must cease
Colours fade and withering winter come—
    Yet say, even as you droop
And nod down to the roots from which you grow,
    The shadows know
Even as they stretch their fingers on the lawn
No parting's loss when lovers long for dawn.

Seal up, sweet lids, the trembling of damp eyes
    And glistening cheeks;
Strength is a beauty only known in grief:
    Like men at war
Who find true comradeship in cruelty
    And bravery
Even as they mourn the very friends they kill,
So may this night of parting bind us still.

FOR GEORGINA

Laughing little buttercup
  Sunbeam of the meadows
Ear of wheat among the corn
  Fledgling of the hedgerows

Mimic of the open air
  Seeking the way the wind went
Stern to escape, swift to return
  Fearlessly dependent

May you ever hide and skip
  By Cherwell or by Granta
Innocent as you are now
  My golden-haired enchanter.

THE STATUES

Bless the baby by your side!
Though the child's not yet conceived
In my dream it was perceived
Etched out in the future's mist
Just as though a calling bell
Told a lonely boat "All's well!"
Silver-clear across a bay,
It startled me before the day
To reassure with that strong voice
One does not question or resist.
Bless the baby by your side!
So clear a scene could not have lied.

In your lips I saw a song
Which at first I could not read—
Recondition was my need,
Yet such scholarship was wrong
For the words were simply said,
"Lay you down your milky head,
Tuck your hands inside the shawl
And may darkness never fall
On that world behind those lights
That bless my days and wake my nights.
Sleep you in your innocence,
Your gull-soft cheeks my recompense."

Dark had just begun to lift
Yet the trees were not awake
Nor had day done more than break.
Spiders slept in dripping webs
Draped across damp windowsills,
Yet beyond the Cumnor hills
The clarity of dream remained.
The more I looked the more engrained
It grew upon my waking mind:
Two shaped rocks left as the sea ebbs—
A slender woman's sleeping form,
A watcher waiting in the dawn.

BELLS
for Edmund

The dog-rose and the wayside poppy tell
The traveller the path they know so well.
They wave and catch his eye as if to say
"We'll stroll with you a measure of the way,
No matter though our stems dig in the ground,
Our scent and colour distance will confound;
And while the sun stipples this lazy brook
We'll loiter on the air to tease a backward look."

Bells ring across the meadows, and the boys
Spill out of school with scrambling whoops of noise
Scampering, scuffling, heads held under arms,
Barking up dogs across the distant farms.
June becomes jeopardy for fish and tree.
A boy's stick scythes the hedge with artistry,
The unmarked poppy and the dog-rose sprawl—
And boy and traveller some happiness recall.

June 1966

THE TRUTH

By the toccata of this autumn's wane
By all this headstrong girasole of leaf
By the bare winter truth none will remain
When the fanged frost has split the frozen sheaf
By this fen's ploughed vernacular of weeds
I bring you permanence, as all recedes.

We know that in few fleeting years mankind will be no more
The barrel of humanity run dry, the grain crushed on a granite floor
We know that in man's evolution lies his fatal flaw.

Yet, in this empire of necessity,
Of ravaged autumn preluding the spring,
Of mock heroic man's effrontery
Cradling extinction, permanence can sing:
Season outlives the species, yet is evanescent too;
Only perception of this fact and suffering are true.

HOSPITAL DAWN

So the pulse beats and slows,
The daylight seeps, creeping
Crosswise against the bandage of the mind
Miraculously lightening
Load upon nodal nerve of lid-red eyes
Fluttering, like kerbside to a skull
New-dashed in crash, not yet abed and cold.

So the revulsion glows
Sky-blind, and it must feel its way along
The daily parapet, nor yet
Look down, nor up, nor yet perceive at all,
So small
That mental island we call sanity.

THE BALLAD OF BRENDAN BEHAN

Come gather round me sweethearts,
　And lovers, lift your heads;
Come, old men from the fireside,
　And children from your beds;
Come neighbours, friends, and travellers
　And hear me sing a stave
Of a laughing boy from Dublin
　Now lying in his grave.

For Brendan loved his city,
　The place where he was born,
He'd toast her health in Mooney's
　From twilight round till morn;
From morn again to twilight
　He'd laugh and sing and say
"Mock all the world, my darlin's,
　But back the I.R.A."

They put him into prison
　When he was fair fifteen,
And innocent of whiskey,
　And only knew potheen:
In Liverpool they locked him
　For smuggling contraband,
For forging of a passport,
　And fighting for his land.

Eight long years being over
　The Borstal boy was free;
He kissed the screws and sold his shoes
　To sail the homeward sea.
He quenched his English prison thirst
　With English prison pay,
And wrote a laughing prison book,
　And then a hanging play.

Joan Littlewood in London
 She sent a telegram:
"Come join us in our theatre,
 Come back me darlin' man!"
Soon Brendan's name is blazoned
 In flashing neon lights.
The laughing boy buys drinks for all
 Throughout the winter nights.

He scribbled as he gargled
 Another singing play,
About a cockney soldier
 Shot by the I.R.A.
His fame crossed the Atlantic,
 His laughter shook New York:
But still he loved his Dublin,
 His Galway and his Cork.

A Gaelic baby daughter
 Grinned up a newborn smile
"Be Jasus! I'll forsake the malt
 And take up milk awhile."
He snatched his pen, and wrote again
 Two books about his friends,
Then quaffed a can at The Shaky Man
 To join and make amends.

Oh, all you wives and lovers
 Take heed unto my tale;
Follow the fate of the laughing boy
 Locked in an English gaol.
The boy with laughter in his eyes,
 And liquor in his veins:
And love like him, forgive like him
 Till Death knocks out your brains.

Courtesy of Anglia T.V.
Transmission 20th March 1964

WEST COAST BLUES

I've tried so many women since I left you,
I've tried so many ways to ease my mind;
I've left my bed to drift through San Diego,
But everything I do I always find

The cold hands of the clock drag oh so slowly
Dead conversations stifle out the day
And nobody's body answers like your body
Nothing can light me up the way you say

"I love you" when you wake up in the morning
A naked lily crumpled in a sheet
"I love you" when your lips hang moist and open—
All I can think of in this rain-washed street

As I drag the boulevards of San Diego
Or wander round the San Francisco Bay
Draining down screwdrivers in topless Broadway
Through Go-Go Mardi Gras I hear you say

"I love you" to the man who lies beside you
Or strokes your hair beside the rhythm band
"I love you" to the man who fills my absence
Hangs up your dress and takes you by the hand.

I've strayed down Sunset Strip to watch the mountains
When it's just not worth while to go to bed;
Within an hour the motel's serving breakfast.
All I can think of are the words you said

The night before I left for San Diego
The night I held your wildness in my arms
The night you showed me all the ways to love you
And paralysed my heart from others' charms.

I've worn away my voice with too much smoking
I've worn away my heels with wasting time
Anesthetized my brain with all-night drinking
But, Wild Delight, all's dust until you're mine.

EAST COAST CALYPSO

Kennedy Airport's bright and gay
Pink floodlight fountains make it look like day
Everybody's rich and kissing and plush
But down on the waterfront—hush! hush! hush!
    New York, New York, slice of life
    When you taste it take a fork and knife
    Central Park's a peculiar place
    And violence smiles with a virgin's face.

Empire State Building's very tall
They say that it sways in a rainy squall;
Janitor tells me since he began
"Fifteen fellas ha' jumped to a man."
    New York, New York . . .

Busy Manhattan's very neat
Gardens and ice-rink along the street
Down in the subway out of sight
No spitting's allowed while the dagos fight.
    New York, New York . . .

Teachers in Harlem after dark
Never look round when they hear a bark.
Keep to the sidewalk away from the wall!
Or your wife won't recognize you at all.
    New York, New York . . .

Greenwich Village is full of charm
Fashion and Painting walk arm in arm,
Your Father's Moustache draws nostalgic tears—
But how did that news vendor lose his ears?
    New York, New York . . .

Sunday last I paid my way
All up the line to Pelham Bay
Walked in the sunshine to something draped
A Bronx kid sobbing that she's been raped.
    New York, New York . . .

71

Taxi driver, he talks to me
Says that he'll take me for a fee
Down to the Chase Manhattan Bank
The back seat's soiled where a junkie stank.
New York, New York . . .

Romantic skyline, Long Island Sound,
Atlantic Ocean, they're all around;
Mightiest city crowned by the sun
Where squirrels and human blood both run.

New York, New York, slice of life
When you taste it take a fork and knife
Central Park's a peculiar place
And violence smiles with a virgin's face.

15th April 1967

SONG FROM "EMBLEMS"

Beneath this scalp within this skin a skull
Out of which peer two globes that clutch the light
A dropped jaw parts two lips and nostril holes
Rake in the pollen of a July night.

Red bones that clasp a book pull white in sinews
Nails protrude to gather up the dust
The valve-fed engine thrums its tambourine
To galvanize a vagrant's wanderlust.

Home, home immortal breakers urge
Grey mountains open the piper's note
Dusk brings the darkness, embers mark the end
Yet what contortion leaps the thrush's throat?

PERENNIA

PERENNIA

For Mary

Only by looking towards the Beyond as the true goal
of ecstasy can man become balanced in the present.
*Balance depends on ecstasy.**   Edgar Wind

I

I stretched and lay beside the stepping-stones
Down on the grass beneath a rowan tree,
And watched the sunlight's warm September tones
Tinge a contented, droning bumblebee
Who buzzed to where a wine-filled blackberry
Had rolled beneath a fallen cock of hay.
Colourful berries hung the hedge by me
Sparkling like daylight glowworms, small and gay;
Hawthorn and hips and haws danced in this sunshine day.

II

The river idled in among the weeds,
Eddying round each obstacle that came,
And lulled the sycamore's slow falling seeds
That fluttered down to make a teasing game
For hungry minnows, searching for a grain
Or water-fly. The clouds born in the stream
Drank in the sunlight and threw back again
Flashes of warmth from where cool trout and bream
Slept while the liquid music murmured through their dream.

III

Soaring aloft in the windswept blue of the sky
Climbing and plunging over the humpbacked air,
Swallows swept and signalled their twittering cry
Over the sun-turned treetop branches where
The streambound dragonfly would never dare
Venture, but hides from his fork-tailed enemy,
Flashing his myriad colours through the clear
Ripples down to the fishes' sanctuary,
Far from the swallows' spontaneous trill of ecstasy.

Pagan Mysteries in the Renaissance (London: Faber & Faber, 1958), p. 53.

IV

A steady wind went rustling through the trees
And swayed the beeches by the river brink,
Combing a cloud of gold and copper leaves
Across the sun, making it dance and blink,
Settling at last to float away, or sink.
And here, away from London and the lights,
I lay against this rowan tree to think
Of things remote from Piccadilly sights—
The Eros statue traffic and the throbbing nights.

V

Scent from the fields around, the rich, brown nuts
Under the chestnut trees, far barley sheaves
With pheasants stalking in the stubble ruts,
Dandelion seeds blown on the rustling breeze,
The clover buzzing with the busy bees,
Feel of the sheep-cropped grass beneath my palm,
The lapping of the water—all of these,
Soothing my mind like some old mystic charm,
Begged me unpack my flute to join their harmless balm.

VI

Then, as I played, gentle flute music came
From all the hill around in soft reply:
The breeze grew stiffer now, and drops of rain
Fell sprinkling from the cloud-flecked summer sky.
I piped more loudly, and the wind grew high,
Billowing blackened mountains through the air
Until the birds had all begun to fly
For shelter to the leafy squirrel's lair,
Showering ivy sprigs, which settled in my hair.

VII

I crouched and played yet more, and still the wind
Thickened and drove the falling leaves in whirls,
Racing them round and round till they were pinned
Beneath a stone or tree-trunk, or in furls
Were hurled to where the savage water curls
His waves against an elm log in the mud,
Banking the leaves in dams against the swirls
And torrents of the overflowing flood,
Pounding the wind and waters' music through my blood.

VIII

My piping died away, and this rough storm
Suddenly sank to a breath like a song half sung,
Now scarcely stirring teazles with its warm
And whispering wind, dawdling its way among
The rain-filled hedges where the berries hung.
A startled spider dropped, bright wide awake;
But gazing past the twig to which he clung
I saw a woman by a small flood-lake
Weeping into the stream as if her heart would break.

IX

Her long hair hung about her childlike face
Framing it in a waterfall cascade
Of dew-drenched gold, giving a gentle grace
To all her form, down which the sunlight played
With flickering smiles while to the stream she prayed:
"Why has the cruel wind carried me here
Away, alone today when, had I stayed,
I should have been a bride?   What did it fear?
Help me to understand, full stream, so calm and clear."

X

The steady river ran without a pause,
But from an acorn hedge a cricket hopped
And, waiting for a while crouched on all fours,
He sprang into her hand as though he'd dropped
From nowhere.   She, surprised and happy, stopped
Her tears, slowly turning her eyes to find
A nearby branch, and on the fork she propped
Her arm and waited.   Then the cricket chimed,
"You have been worshipped more than may your humankind.

XI

"Wild animals and insects, brooks and birds
Have listened for your name in every sound
And sung it through the air.   The goats and herds
Of sheep and cows have sent your name around
The hills until they echoing rebound
With wafted paeans to your beauty, praised
Till all the natural orchestra is drowned
In echoes flooding back, and all are dazed
Crying, 'Perennia!   Perennia!' amazed.

XII

"You have been carried by the wind, unseen,
And set away from cheering crowds apart;
For Hespera, the jealous Goddess Queen,
By you has lost her rule over Man's heart:
And she who smooths the oceans and can chart
The wandering planets' courses will not bear
One who will rival her, with power to start
Spring fires of love in mortals everywhere;
And harsh the punishment she cries on those who dare.

XIII

"But in this place, beside this wooded bank,
You will be safe awhile."   Then he was gone
Back to his hedge before she tried to thank
Her mentor: and, thinking herself alone,
She slipped the crumpled dresses she had on,
Standing reflected in the limpid pool;
And treading gently on a stepping-stone,
Fanned by the sun, she felt the water cool
Her feet while shoals of fishes swam by in a school.

XIV

Slowly she slipped her sunlit body in,
Parting the stream which strayed around her limbs
Washing her loosened hair and tender skin,
While she bathed as the lazy goldfish swims,
Or as the long-legged summer insect skims
The idle surface as he drinks his fill
From pools and shallows where the water brims
Its sides; so like a water lily still
She turned and floated soon forgetting all her ill.

XV

And cooled, refreshed and softened by the brook,
She climbed upon the bank and closed her eyes
To lie and feel the sun, or gazed to look
Up at the wisps of cloud and butterflies
Fluttering to and fro, while high birds' cries
Warn them that they must leave their happy play,
Brushing the dreamy heat-haze where she dries
Her slender body.   So the sun's warm ray
Caressed her sleeping, streamwashed figure where she lay.

80

XVI

Soon down the winding, wooded hillside track
A boyish figure with a bow appeared
Searching into the sun, his head thrown back
Showing a face that wore as yet no beard;
Whose hair fell loose like sheep's wool newly sheared
Across his neck: he unsuspecting came
To where she lay asleep; and stopped, and peered,
Scarcely believing that her face and frame
Could be so beautiful and yet remain the same.

XVII

Entranced he gazed, his goatskin slung across
His body while he stood and wondered long
Whether this creature sleeping on the moss,
Warmed by the sun and lulled by insects' song
Was mortal or a goddess to belong
In such tranquil surroundings; if some freak
Of Nature had united weak with strong
To make perfection. Aching now to speak,
Yet fearful to disturb her rest, he kissed her cheek.

XVIII

As yet too young to know his archery,
His heart was filled with love of purest fire
And all his soaring spirits, once so free,
Were anchored now in innocent desire
To share with her the cheerful chaffinch choir
That sang above her head; to hear her laugh;
To trace safe paths across the dangerous mire,
Show her his mountain goats, his tender calf
Newborn, his secret haunts, his new-cut hazel staff.

XIX

She felt the touch upon her cheek and saw
The boy-god's face a moment over her
So brilliant that she blinked; but saw no more,
For he had vanished without sound or stir
Seeing her eyes were mortal, that they were
Unable to look safely on a god.
But as he vanished a small tuft of fur
Fell from his goatskin where his hazel rod
Had rubbed. She took it, shaking off a sleepy nod.

XX

Heavy with rest she looked about again
And saw all as it was before she slept;
But now her breast filled with a yearning pain
To see the man whose image still she kept
Before her eyes, and mirrored teardrops crept
Down her smooth cheeks to fall into the tide.
But as she clasped the fur and softly wept
A robin hopped his way close by her side
And quizzically waited till her eyes were dried.

XXI

Then birds of all descriptions gathered round
At peace with one another—hedge-sparrows
And bunting, wrens and larks flew to the ground
Fearlessly mingling with the hawks and crows.
Ibis and lapwing spread their summer shows
Of multicoloured feathers, and with these
Peregrine falcons from far Iceland snows
And eagles from the golden Pyrenees
Settled upon a branch or circled round her knees.

XXII

And animals of many breeds and kinds,
Rabbits and does, foxes and water-voles,
Hedgehogs and donkeys, kingly stags and hinds,
Earthworms and beetles, blindly burrowing moles
Pushed through their tunnels or crept from their holes,
Or travelled from thick forests and wide parks
To see her with their young—mares with their foals,
Goats bringing kids with strange, distinctive marks,
And sheepdogs guiding lambs and sheep with careful barks.

XXIII

Now all of nature seemed to hold its breath.
Not a leaf stirred. A moorhen's feathers brushed
A stone and paused. The air was quiet as death.
The river that awhile before had rushed
In torrents hesitated and was hushed.
No creature moved. An ivy-covered oak
Older than all the forest, with trunks crushed
And torn by many a furious tempest, broke
The silence and at last to this great crowd he spoke.

XXIV

"Perennia will live amongst us, free
To make her peace here. Let her never lack
Shelter or food, clothing or company.
When she calls music, echoes will blow back
Your bird-songs from hill-hollows till they pack
The sunbeams full of sounds. When she needs food
Fetch her ripe nuts and let small squirrels crack
Them for her. Mice, bring hedge-wine newly brewed,
And birds of prey, protect her as your tender brood.

XXV

"These hillslopes, lady, and this cave are yours
Where every night Eros, unseen, will come
To be your close companion when the moors
And ditches shudder, when the kestrels shun
The treetops and the badger's feet are numb.
And, when the tender corn shoots in the stalk
And you are warmed by the fresh April sun,
Eros will laugh with you and share your talk
When after dew-filled days you make your homeward walk.

XXVI

"All here is yours, and though you may not see
His godlike body he will not be far."
Then with these words the old, majestic tree
Ceased as the early, brightest evening star
Shone in the sky. The grey bat and nightjar
Rose from their perches. Softly, wave on wave,
They all departed without trace or scar
Left on the ground. She watched the last rook brave
The cool night air, then stood and peered into the cave.

XXVII

Flickering of ten thousand glowworm cells
Shadowed the floor and shone upon the walls,
And tiny sounds from comfrey and harebells
Mingled with music spun from waterfalls
That splashed the sides of inner rock-hewn halls
Where malachite and agate, amethyst,
Fluorspar and bluejohn, jades, opals,
Topaz and lapis lazuli were kissed
By wistful perfumes till her eyes were full of mist.

XXVIII

And then more lovely than a well-played lute
The voice of Eros spoke beside her ear
Telling her to go in and eat the fruit
That lay upon the table, and to cheer
Herself with honey-mead, the country beer;
And tell him all that she had felt that day;
To lie down on the bed of maiden-hair
And spend the hours in happiness and play
Of childish innocence while he beside her lay.

XXIX

When first light broke the boy-god sadly strayed
Into the forest while Perennia
Slept on the ferns within the cavern shade.
But on the farther shore now calling her
By name, the voice of salt Salacia,
Her elder sister, woke her from deep sleep
With calling through the misty morning air.
She wrapped a silk about her form to keep
It dry from dew and ran to where the willows weep.

XXX

"O strong West Wind, carry my sister here
As you did me," she begged. "Set her beside
These willow trees. Warm her that we may cheer
And rest her well after the weary ride
In search of me; lift her across this tide!"
Obediently the West Wind took his load
And brought Salacia in one gust-stride
Across to where the folded daisies stowed
Away their secrets till the morning cocks had crowed.

XXXI

When she saw all the joy of this demesne,
The natural happiness this valley held,
Plenty and peace beyond all she had seen
In years of travel, then her heart rebelled
Till jealousy beneath her eyelids welled:
Yet she contrived to cover her disgrace
Probing with artful questions, which compelled
Her sister to describe the god and place,
And tell at last that she had only glimpsed his face.

XXXII

"Sweet sister," soon she smiled, "this luxury
Of animals and birds for retinue
May fascinate; but can your Eros be
So radiant that he must hide from you
In stealthy midnight visitings his true
Form? Can he be a pure, immortal child
Such as you say? If he is fine to view,
Why does he hide a body that is mild
And harmless? He may be a beast, gross and defiled.

XXXIII

"For many a satyr has an easy charm
And glowing look, insinuating trust
That merely leads us on to our own harm
Till we are prostituted to its lust
And every passionate and goatish gust
That shudders through its body. Though he fawns
And flatters you with presents, yet you must
Fly from this place before full morning dawns
And listen to the loving voice of one who warns.

XXXIV

"Or if you will not leave this haunted glade,
Tonight, when he is sleeping by your side,
Take up a glowing branch that you had laid
Upon the fire before the embers died,
And by its light destroy your sleeping guide
Before you are disfigured in your turn."
The West Wind blew upon the roughening tide
Making the angry waters boil and churn
And carried back Salacia with buffets stern,

XXXV

And set her down. But she returning heard
Upon this farther bank a hidden sigh
That straying Eros heaved who, deeply stirred
Within his heart, wondered the reason why
His pulse beat restlessly and mouth seemed dry,
And all his sports and pleasures seemed to cloy
After his night spent in the cave nearby
With pure Perennia. She guessed the boy
Who sighed unseen to be her sister's source of joy.

XXXVI

Gently she whispered, "Young god, in distress
When all your kingdom loves to wake and sing—
What is it that disturbs your happiness?
Have you not, with my sister, everything
You could desire? Perhaps some hidden spring
Wells up within to trouble you, although
You cannot yet describe it. Does this bring
You sighing to this bank? If that is so
Come to your loved one's sister: learn what I will show.

XXXVII

"For you must lie by me and kiss me as
You did your own Perennia, and I
Will teach you secrets that the grown man has
But hides from childhood's uncorrupted eye;
And all your misery will pass you by
As golden daybreak floods your youthful heart."
In unsuspecting ignorance of why
Salacia should scheme to make them part
He lay, though still unseen, to learn this lady's art.

XXXVIII

A mighty vision burst within her head
As mortal with immortal were combined.
She dreamed she saw a flying waggon led
By two great horses and controlled behind
By Eros tugging at the reins, confined
Within his chariot. The right-hand horse
Was white as snow and knew the driver's mind:
The black one plunged and reared up in its course
Dragging its driver down with devastating force.

XXXIX

Then blasted with milk of eternity
Her body scattered in a thunderflash
Over the hillslopes far out to the sea;
And Eros, knowing all, fled with the crash
Back to Perennia lest she should dash
Terrified into danger: but the trees
Protected her; the river would not splash
Her where she sat, with mushrooms on her knees
Gathered while waiting for his absent melodies.

XL

Now loving her beyond all other things,
As he returned and found her sitting still
Upon the tree-stump near their cave, his wings
Grew weary, and he roamed with her until
The sun went down and she had played her fill
Among the hedges, searching every briar
For berries: then, when all the glade grew still
And owls flew low, she turning to retire
Within their cave lay down and rested by the fire.

XLI

Though he had learned the cause of his strange pain
The night before, he was content to lie
In innocence with her and to refrain
From any harm, afraid lest she should die
Delirious. He whispered songs to try
To soothe her tender body into sleep:
And to his softly spoken lullaby
She dozed upon the yielding fern-moss heap
As round the cave the shadows lengthened and grew deep.

XLII

In unmistrusting love and simple faith
Eros slept wrapped in darkness from all sight:
But in her dreams there hovered like a wraith
The figure of a satyr such as might
Haunt dying men on execution night.
She woke in horror and lay still as stone
Watching the embers glow. Then, by their light,
She stretched to reach a branch that lay alone
Kindling within a cave-draught where the night had blown.

XLIII

She lifted up the brand in breathless stealth:
It faded low. She blew, and a bright spark
Flew like a comet showing all the wealth
And beauty of his body through the dark
Falling to burn his shoulder with a mark
That seared into the skin. Then he was gone:
And she collapsed in sorrow for her stark
Betrayal of his love, and fell upon
Her lonely bed and wept until the daylight shone.

XLIV

Eros meanwhile, under his mother's care
Had been plucked back to heaven when the burn
Singed, and was held in close confinement there
Until entirely healed, for his stern
Mother determined he should not return
To earth again till her competitor
In beauty was destroyed. She watched him yearn
For her companionship and sought the more
To cauterize his love and pay her ancient score.

XLV

She meditated how the wind had seized
Perennia upon her wedding day
At her command, and now, with thoughts diseased
By jealousy, she saw that while away
Her son had saved her victim; and their play
Of adolescent love had brought more true
Joy and contentment to this child of clay
That ordinary mortals ever knew.
Then in her mind dreams of retaliation grew.

XLVI

Pondering on a strange and fitting task
To lay upon her, one that seemed beyond
All human power, she sent a dove to ask
Perennia to enter in a bond
Of friendship. In return she could respond
By searching all the riverbed to count
The hairs upon the lily-stalks. This fond,
Obedient dove flew earthwards to recount
Her message as the crescent moon began to mount.

XLVII

The falling moonbeams made the pebbles shine
White in the pools and shallows as she heard
The bitter task that Hespera in fine
And flattering phrases sent her by this bird.
She stared down where a water spider stirred
Beneath the surface near his bubble trap,
Seeing her own reflection miniatured
Within his airy prison, while the lap
Of water seemed so pure she felt her mind would snap.

XLVIII

A newt disturbed a clump of meadow-sweet
And peered through clusters of marsh-marigold
To catch a caddis-fly. His weblike feet
Darted round crowfoot stems to find a hold,
Or paused among those loosestrife buds which fold
The purple flowers close within their leaves
To shield them from night vapours and the cold.
She watched him jerk and scamper by degrees
On to a full-lipped lily, where he seemed to freeze.

XLIX

She started up. Along the water's edge
Thousands of tiny creatures had appeared:
Lizards and newts crawled from the willow-sedge,
And daphnia and water-boatmen steered
Among the traces water-mites had cleared.
Fat bullfrogs made their way, with brook lamprey
And softest moths blown from the old-man's-beard
To settle on this lily carpetry,
While fishes searched the mud and depths they could not see.

L

Then, understanding that the friendliness
Of this grey, moonlit host united here
Was all to save her from the bitterness
Of Hespera, she cried away her fear
In sobs of joy; and when the newt drew near
Giving the answer that the Queen required
She sang her gratitude in tones so clear
It seemed the waterfalls had all conspired
To hold her love-filled melody when she retired.

LI

Hespera heard her answer, but in hate
Ordered a second task—that she should send
An apple plucked from where grey, desolate
Crags on the mountain towered to contend
With piling clouds; determined so to bend
This mortal's will, and break her in a test
Of such immensity, that in the end
Death would be prayed for as a welcome guest
Before the climbing sun had settled in the West.

LII

Waking within the lonely cavern mouth
Perennia saw gillyflowers blow
Beside the river. Then from out the South
A speck came flying, and she watched it grow
Until the dove flew down to let her know
Its message. With a torn, half-stifled cry
She let her tears of desperation flow
Praying that distant Eros would be by
To give her his forgiveness if she was to die.

LIII

But from her side a golden eagle soared
Into the sun to find the fruit for her,
And circling where the precipices roared
Severed the apple for Perennia,
Flying in feathered bold regalia
Northwards again to lay it at her feet.
She sent the dove with this ambrosia
Back to its cruel mistress; and to greet
The mighty bird's return fed him raw flesh to eat.

LIV

The Queen of Beauty would not rest until
Her unoffending rival had been killed,
Or broken utterly beneath her will,
Ordering now the fire should be twice filled
With coals and branches till the cave was grilled
In heat unbearable, and all that night,
While natural life beneath the moon was stilled,
The child should stay within the furnace light
Locked in a blaze that made the metalled rocks unite.

LV

A thousand silkworms spun a thick cocoon
Over her body, and the phoenix came
To give her courage from his magic tune,
While ancient salamanders, blind and lame,
Gave her their power to withstand the flame—
Secret for untold weary centuries.
She tremblingly endured the pain and shame
Through crawling hours that stretched eternities,
Till release came at last with morning's certainties.

LVI

The unrelenting goddess now designed
One hazard more for her to undergo:
She must descend into the grave to find
And bring back Beauty from the world below,
Beyond that stream where lethal waters flow,
Venturing to the kingdom of the shades.
No living mortal had been known to row
Across that river twice, and in those glades
Of chalklike soil no nightingale's clear serenades

LVII

Disturbed the silent kingdom of the dead.
Perennia was stunned into a trance
Of horrified amazement. Through her head
Imaginary phantoms seemed to dance—
One leering with a gross, malicious glance,
Another gaping through an earth-filled skull
At her—and as she watched them grin and prance
She turned to die rather than try to cull
Trophies from lands where even gods grew pale and dull.

LVIII

Her gentle river, that had washed her heart
So many times with music of content,
Would surely understand, and take her part
While she dissolved her body, and prevent
The suffering that drowned souls underwent.
This river knew her thoughts and, with a stir
That hardly rippled, asked her to relent,
Taking upon the quest that piece of fur
That Eros, when he first appeared, had left with her.

LIX

Holding it in her hand she strayed that day
Where scythes and sickles had been left to rot
As though the reapers had been called away
Suddenly, leaving all within that spot
Carelessly unattended and forgot.
She gathered and arranged them round an elm
Which wreathed its twisted branches in a knot
That masked a gong, spreading to overwhelm
The entrance of a path to the infernal realm.

91

LX

With an unearthly courage she went on,
Coming to where a ferryboat was moored
Near to a landing stage, its rudder gone.
She tore a piece of fur and stepped on board
Giving it to the guide who was restored
To thoughts of love and youth on touching it.
And when the journey on the bitter ford
Was passed, Perennia bestowed a bit
On every beast that blocked her entry to the pit.

LXI

At last she viewed the splendours of the grave,
The terrifying and majestic scene
Where all the souls of the departed wave
Rank upon rank, far as the eyes can glean
A glimmering of twilight. Here the Queen
Of Night sat high enthroned above the throng
Knowing the mortal's errand, having seen
Her journey down, and followed it along
The labyrinthine paths beyond the midnight gong.

LXII

The Queen gave her a casket with the words
That it should not be opened. But when she
Returned, as she had come, to where sleek herds
Of cattle grazed beneath the wych-elm tree,
And saw again all nature's artistry,
She longed to take some beauty from the case
To win her Eros back again, that he
Loving her would forgive all her disgrace.
She opened it; and fell like death upon her face.

LXIII

The little mist of beauty had enclosed
Her vital spirits till she lay so cold
That all her living kingdom round supposed
Their mistress dead. Ravens and night owls tolled
Their evensong, and sad marsh marigold
Lowered their petalled heads to touch the brook
While clouds across the sun seemed to enfold
The world in mourning till it made it look
As though the tears of life were in each leaf that shook.

LXIV

But Eros, now recovered from his burn,
Yearning to see Perennia once more
Watched for a moment when he might return
Unnoticed by his mother, to restore
The laughter that her eyes had held before
When both together they had mocked the rain,
Slept in the sun and run along the shore
Like young gazelles, untouched by hate or pain,
Resting only to wake to happiness again.

LXV

He came back to the stream—but all was changed.
No birds, no animals bathed in the sun.
Where herds of sheep and goats before had ranged
Browsing within the meadows, now not one
Appeared. The very fishes seemed to shun
The surface where the lily-leaves were spread
In rich profusion. Silence seemed to stun
His senses. Then, by where the elm tree shed
Its leaves he saw his love lying as one struck dead.

LXVI

And yet no agony was in her face:
Beauty had calmed her brow in perfect peace.
The harshest sufferings had left no trace
Upon her cheeks, for sleep had brought release
From all her miseries, and made them cease.
Unutterable love surged in his heart
As bending down, and taking off his fleece
To cover her, he saw her earthly part
Outshone the brightest miracle of heaven's art.

LXVII

He brushed away the mist with gentle breath;
Then, trembling in her eyes, she saw him stand
In all his radiance. The sleep of death,
The great descent into that other land
From which no man returns, the tasks, the brand
Were over now. She gazed with steadfast eyes
Upon her love, who raised her by her hand.
The whole of nature burst to life with cries
Of rapture, and Perennia cried to the skies:

I have danced, with eternity dawning,
        lain between delicate petals of night,
Stroked the blue butterfly-wings of the morning,
        tiptoed the moon on a cobweb of light,
Washed in the waterfall, made my limbs moister,
        tickled a slippery trout by the gills,
Plunged with the otter and yawned with the oyster,
        ridden a stallion over the hills.

Ride on with me to the lands of tomorrow,
        sail where our souls will be sundered no more,
Far from where breakers of parting and sorrow
        pound on the heart like the waves on the shore.

I have run down the rainbow and covered my traces,
        blown on the wind and sung to the sea,
Whispered brave words in the holiest places
        setting the terrible glaciers free,
Taken the sting from the arrogant lightning,
        tied up a maniac murderer's hands,
Lain by the lizard to watch the day brightening,
        burned with the sun on the tropical sands.

Ride on with me to the lands of tomorrow,
        sail where our souls will be sundered no more,
Far from where breakers of parting and sorrow
        pound on the heart like the waves on the shore.

I have cradled the rabbit newborn in the burrow,
        fanned it with down from a kingfisher's crest,
Followed the field-mouse search in the furrow
        pouching up grain to take back to her nest.
Come to a land where the roebucks are bounding,
        pick up a thistle and knock on the sky:
Dance to the fields where the huntsmen are sounding
        the horn of a dawn in which hatred shall die.

Ride on with me to the lands of tomorrow,
        sail where our souls will be sundered no more,
Burst through the bindings of passion and sorrow,
        ride on my heart like the waves on the shore.

And with her song still ringing in my ears,
I woke beside the Box Hill stepping-stones,
My flute had slipped among some travellers'-tears,
Where in the evening wind brown autumn comes
Dropped through the weeds and made wide, rippling zones.
A bonfire flamed and crackled cheerfully
Scenting the air with smoke, till in my bones
I knew that I had seen reality
Lying upon that bank beneath the rowan tree.

Cambridge, September 1961